How to Plan Services in a Multi-church Setting

John Waller
Rector, The Brickhills and Stoke Hammond
Diocese of Oxford

GROVE BOOKS LIMITED
RIDLEY HALL RD CAMBRIDGE CB3 9HU

Contents

Acknowledgments
Grateful thanks to all my friends in the Group for the Renewal of Worship, and especially to Helen Bent and Coryn Stanforth. Thanks also to Tim Norwood.

First Impression November 2024
ISSN 0144-1728
ISBN 978 1 78827 427 2

Introduction

1

Sunday Services

Week	Great Tremlett	Little Tremlett	Woodby	Woodby Chapel End	Grilsby on the Hill
1	8am Communion (*July at Little Tremlett*)	9.15 Lord's Supper (*July at Great Tremlett*)	11am Songs of Praise (*from Easter to Harvest*)	4pm Evensong (*sung on alternate months*)	6pm Compline (*3pm in Winter*)
2	9.15 Communion with Parade Service (*except when it is Morning Prayer*)	8.15 am BCP Communion (*ASB between 1980-2000*)	11.30 Rock 'n' Roll Church (*1950s style*) 21:19 Vespers	10 am Communion (*Eucharist in alternate months*)	9 am All Age Service (*BCP Matins if no children*)
3	8 am Communion; 11.15 High Mass (*CW*)	9.22 All Age Eucharist	12 noon Messy Communion	6.10pm Service of the Word with Communion (*whispered in the Spring months*)	4.15pm Taizé worship (*subject to resolution of Copyright battle*)
4	10.08 am Modern Worship (*Quire practice on the preceding Friday, 8pm*)	8 am Holy Communion (*unless it's cold*)	11.15 Holy Communion (*in the school if the month has an "R" in it*)	9am Lord's Supper (*Holy Communion in March and November*) 12 noon Parade	8 am Holy Communion; 10 am Morning Worship; 6pm Evensong; 9pm Compline
5	9.45 "All Together" (*January,April, August, November*)	"All Together" (*February, June, October*)	9.45 "All Together" (*March if the year number is even, September*)	9.45 "All Together" (*March if the year number is odd, July, December*)	11am Family Worship

Children's work: at any service starting between 9 and 11.17, except Woodby Chapel End. Assuming any children turn up. Excluding summer, Xmas, Easter and half-term holidays, and days when there is a Church Parade at Great Tremlett (but not Woodby)

A few years ago a small book was published entitled *Writes of the Church,* which used the framework of an imagined church magazine letters' page to shed a humorous light on some of the quirks and oddities of church life, through (as the subtitle says) the 'gripes and grumbles of people in the pews.'[1] On an associated website that promoted the book there is a chart for a monthly pattern of services for that fictitious group of five churches, which we have reproduced on the previous page.[2] This displays a bewildering variety of service times, and many different descriptions of services, with no less than four different titles for Holy Communion, and a sometimes bizarre selection of other services. All the factors that affect where, and when, a service might actually take place, or have any provision for children, are sometimes hard to follow. Of course it is all exaggerated for comic effect, but some aspects of this chart might look horribly familiar to some of us who have to wrestle with real and complex service patterns for groups of churches on a regular basis.

My training for ordained ministry some years ago mostly assumed the simple setting of 'one parish, one church, one vicar,' but in all my time in full-time ministry I have only spent five years in that kind of setting. Most of my ministry has involved the major and constant challenge of maintaining and revising the pattern of church services across a benefice or group of churches, and frequently or even constantly revising and adapting that pattern to a greater or lesser extent. Recently, the gradual return to face-to-face worship after COVID-19 raised a particular challenge to be open to continuing change and flexibility. Most churches went through various intermediate stages on the journey back towards the previous normality, and at some point we all had to decide whether or not to return to the pattern of services as it had been before. However, as I look back over all my years in ministry, I cannot recall a substantial discussion with other clergy and ministers about this subject, or any clear opportunity to reflect together on the ways in which we have tried to manage this aspect of our work.

This booklet is offered to incumbents and other clergy, lay ministers, as well as Parochial Church Councils (PCCs) and others in leadership roles, who might be involved in planning and revising patterns of services for groups of churches. In the second chapter I will give three particular examples from different contexts, summarizing how they have planned and changed their service patterns, and noting some of the factors that have shaped their approach. Then in the third chapter I will identify and discuss a number of the issues and questions that might arise in relation to our patterns of services. In the fourth chapter I will briefly explore some achievable and creative opportunities to try some new and different things in the context of an ongoing extensive pattern of services, and then finally offer some concluding thoughts.

2

Some Examples

In this chapter I offer three examples of the contexts for patterns of services in different local settings, along with some indications of how the patterns might change over time. They are substantially based on the experiences of real clergy, churches and parishes. The first example is a fairly simple group of churches in small villages, while the second is a rather more complex ecumenical partnership in a new urban area, which raises some particular issues which are relevant in such a setting. The third example is a more extensive group of rural parishes in a challenging setting.

These examples cannot cover all the possible settings as, for example, we have not looked in detail at urban churches that hold multiple services, and might have multiple congregations using one church building. Also, these examples are primarily focused on Anglican churches, although there is ecumenical involvement in some of them, and we have not tried to address the situation of churches in very different contexts in other parts of the world, where various practical challenges might be much greater than anything we face in this country. However, we hope that these examples will be sufficient to raise a variety of issues that will be explored further in the next chapter.

Example 1: A Group of Village Churches

Over twenty years ago, this group of three Church of England churches serving small village communities had a fourth village and church added to the group, at around the time that a new incumbent was appointed. With this expansion, the pattern of services needed to be reviewed and changed, as the previous pattern that had been used by the three churches would not be sustainable with a fourth church added to the group. The new incumbent initially asked for the current patterns to be sustained for a time (with some extra help from visiting clergy and lay leaders), so that he could experience and understand the current pattern of the four churches, before beginning a review process that would lead to any changes.

Over the next year, there was discussion at the regular meeting of churchwardens and ministers, before a proposed new pattern was prepared and offered to the four PCCs to be considered. Some PCCs made more effort than others to involve a wider group of church members in the discussion. Eventually, a new pattern, with some changes from the original proposal, was agreed. This was based around services usually taking place every week in all four of the churches, with the only exception being a joint service for all four churches that was held when there was a fifth Sunday in the month. Service times were mainly at 9.30am and 11am, but there were others at 6pm, and just a few at 8am and 4pm as well.

The intention was to offer a variety of styles of worship during the month in each church. In this pattern the incumbent was normally leading three services each Sunday, along with occasional help from retired clergy, and those who had Permission to Officiate (PTO). Most services used the lectionary readings, so often some of the same preparation could be used for more than one service, but had to be applied to very different contexts. For example, a typical Sunday might involve the incumbent preparing to lead and preach at a Communion service and then a family service from the same theme and readings, and then to prepare to preach at evensong with a different set of readings.

A typical Sunday might involve the incumbent preparing a communion service, a family service and then Evensong

There was one Reader leading services regularly across all the churches, along with some other lay people who led services occasionally. Another challenge was to provide musical resources for all the services. Apart from one 8.00am said Communion each month, the hope was to have an organist at all the other services, and this was often possible, although it became more difficult over time, as the number of available organists and keyboard players reduced. At this time there were choirs in two of the four churches, and they supported some of the services each month, often the more traditional ones.

The new pattern was reviewed and checked after twelve months, but no significant changes were made.

About ten years later, the pattern was reviewed again, by a similar process of discussion, along with a questionnaire that all church members were invited to fill in. As can happen with such a consultation exercise, this produced a wide variety of preferences and opinions, but there was no clear consensus that emerged. As a result of the discussions, there was some reduction in the number of services, more for some churches than for others, as the aim of every church having the same number of services each month was now given up, because it was hard to sustain, and no longer seemed to be the correct priority.

An attempt was also made to make some changes to service times, moving earlier services from 9.30am to 9.00am, while leaving later services at 11.00am. The intention was to allow ministers more time for pastoral care through conversation with attenders and then for travel between services, but this did not last for very long, as most people soon preferred to go back to 9.30am, when the new pattern was reviewed after twelve months. The incumbent was now usually taking two services each Sunday, acknowledging the reality that, in addition to these, there were frequently one or more extra services, along with other church or village events that often happened on Sundays as well.

In the years since the previous review the musical resources available had gradually changed. The two choirs had amalgamated into one benefice choir, with the aim of supporting worship across all the churches, although in practice they tended to take part in more services in the two churches that had previously had choirs of their own, and not very often at the other two churches. A music group had started, which always played for one of the family services, and sometimes for other joint services and events. Over time the pool of available organists gradually reduced, and the benefice came to rely mainly on one person for most of the services, which was a heavy load for one person to carry. While there was still a hope to have an organist or keyboard player at all services, this was not always possible, and the congregations got used to singing to recorded musical backing at services from time to time.

Some years later, as regular services were restarted after the COVID-19 lockdown, there was a further revision of the pattern. These changes were made in part because of reducing numbers of regular attenders at some of the services. There was also a particular prompt to change in one village because the Methodist church had recently closed. The two churches in that village had held joint family services for many years, and also occasional joint communion services, so the parish church had to adjust its pattern of services when these joint services came to an end. Also, it seemed to be getting harder to find clergy cover from further afield for Communion services. There were now monthly joint services for the four congregations together. Each church usually had a Communion service and a family service each month, and there was also a variety of other services in some places, as two of the churches were now using community halls in their villages for some family services. Some held some services of Mattins or Evensong, and there were some other non-Communion services, including a regular café church in one village. Most services still used the lectionary readings, but with perhaps more flexibility than in the past, partly to limit the amount of preparation needed by leaders and preachers, and also sometimes, for example at café church, to have a theme and Bible reading that seemed appropriate for the occasion.

It seemed to be getting harder to find clergy cover from further afield for communion services

Example 2: A New Urban Ecumenical Group of Churches

This example follows an ecumenical partnership of churches over a period when new housing was expanding quickly across their extensive parish. Initially the group included two historic village churches in small village communities that were now surrounded by new housing, and there were also two recently built combined church and community centre buildings set in new housing areas. In the next few years, another small older church building, that had been quite isolated amongst woodland and fields, was brought into greater use, as housing was built around it, and there was also a new church primary school established in one of the new communities.

The partnership involved four denominations—Church of England, Methodist, United Reformed Church and Baptist. However, the stipendiary team of clergy only included people from two of those denominations, although ministers from the other denominations did visit to take services from time to time.

A significant factor in the planning of services was that all the services were included in the quarterly plan of services produced by the local Methodist Circuit. This meant that services had to be planned in blocks of three months, and agreed well ahead of each quarter beginning, to meet the Circuit's deadlines for the information they needed. Planning the services for the whole partnership each quarter has always been a complex task, during the regular times, and even more so for major festivals and special occasions.

Over a period of more than twenty years there were various changes, often reflecting the approaches of different clergy who were part of the team. Earlier on each church tended to operate quite independently, largely with their own minister, and the style and character of each church, and service, varied a great deal, some reflecting clear denominational traditions, and others more modern and informal styles. In earlier days the wide variety of service times reflected the relative independence of each church, but later they were standardized to be mainly at 9.30am or 11am, which helped ministers to be able to move around and sometimes lead more than one service. However, one church held to their preferred time of 10am, which did not sit easily with the rest of the pattern. Over time there were more regular joint services, in an attempt to bring the whole partnership together.

Those leading services included the stipendiary clergy, with some support from retired and non-parish clergy, along with authorized lay preachers, and also sometimes members of congregations. All the regular discussions and decisions about plans for services took place in the meetings of the staff team. In earlier years this only included the ordained ministers, but over time it was expanded to include authorized lay ministers as well, and also those who were in training for any form of ministry. There has been a significant challenge in the reduction of clergy posts, while the population of the area continued to grow, and also a reduction of support from partner denominations for the established ecumenical structures in the area.

There has been a significant challenge in the reduction of clergy posts

Other changes over a longer period included changes in the balance of influences on the style of worship as the denominational mix moved from mainly Church of England and United Reformed Church to mainly Church of England and Methodist—increasingly reflecting a circuit rather than a more congregational approach. As clergy became more mobile, the worship style increasingly tended to reflect the style of the visiting clergy rather than the local congregation. For example, one of the changes that perhaps followed from this was that the worship of one congregation became less distinctly Anglican than it had previously been, and they began using an ecumenical liturgy rather than *Common Worship*.

Over time the use of lay ministry first increased and then later declined, as the emphasis of the ministry team swung between a commitment to sustain multiple congregations and a desire for pastoral leadership of each congregation by clergy. There used to be two morning congregations in three of the churches—one traditional, often with Communion, and one 'family' in style. All five church buildings now have one congregation, all holding services at 10am. Perhaps this reflects a desire for fairness, and also the current plan means that clergy are not doing multiple services on a Sunday morning. This means that there are enough worship leaders for there to be one at the service at each church, ensuring that they are able to be available for pastoral contact with worshippers both before and after services.

There have also been interesting debates, not unusual in ecumenical projects of this kind, around the use of individual cups for distributing the wine at Communion, with an Anglican minister at one time refusing to use them, although they reflect the usual practice of some other denominational traditions. Of course this has been discussed much more widely in the light of all the health concerns following COVID-19, and, although individual cups are not officially permitted in the Church of England, a number of churches did use them for a period of time following COVID-19, and some are continuing to do so on an ongoing basis.[3]

One ordained minister who has served in this partnership has reflected that its story might be one of continuing changes of emphasis, between the key factors of the denominational traditions of clergy, the varied expectations of congregations, and the search for cohesion across the whole partnership.

Example 3: A Larger, More Complex Rural Benefice

This example is of a group of eight Church of England parishes joined in a benefice in a rural and coastal area. The benefice covers a considerable area of coastline, with holiday traffic for much of the year, and the challenges of rural roads means that travel between the churches can take a considerable time.

When a new incumbent arrived in the benefice, there was a pattern of services in place which were nearly all timed to begin at 10.30am. Some years previously, there had been a large ministry team of clergy and Licenced Lay Ministers. Normally it can be helpful, when settling in to a new post, to take some time to listen and observe before making any changes. However, in this case the incumbent realized that with virtually all worship beginning at the same time, the pattern in place would only allow her to be in each parish for a Sunday service once every two months, that is, only six times a year.

So the decision was made to write and circulate a paper explaining the difficulties with the current service pattern. Each parish was asked what pattern and type of worship they would ideally like, and how they would be willing to compromise in order to make a whole pattern sustainable. Interestingly, every parish knew what they wanted for themselves, and nobody made any offers to compromise.

A new service pattern was trialled, with assistance from a LLM and a retired member of the clergy from a neighbouring benefice, who agreed each to offer one Sunday a month to the benefice. The pattern that was trialled included two services of Holy Communion each Sunday morning. Morning worship services were then added into the plan so that each church got the number and type of services that they had requested. Churches were placed in pairs so that the two Communion services would happen each Sunday in churches which were geographically close. There were also local factors affecting travel which had to be taken into consideration such as queues of traffic along part of the coast road due to large numbers of parked vehicles.

The majority of parishes wished to have two or three services a month.

The majority of parishes wished to have two or three services a month. One parish has four services a month and one village requested a single service per month. The pattern was initially sustainable. The incumbent led worship in every parish on a monthly basis and the remainder of services were led by Licensed Lay Ministers and Authorized Worship Assistants.

Congregations have been content with the type and number of services. However, service times have proved challenging with complaints arising about services both too early and too late!

However, what seemed like a sustainable pattern was put under strain when several members of the ministry team became unwell and sadly one of the Licensed Lay Ministers died. This produced challenges in filling the rota but other people are coming forward to explore licensed or authorized ministry.

The second part of the plan was to look at broadening the styles of worship offered across the benefice. A benefice service has been introduced for when a fifth Sunday in the month occurred. These joint services involve people from across the benefice in reading the Bible passages, leading intercessions and so on. The incumbent is trying to get good visiting preachers to these benefice services to give them more of a sense of occasion. Refreshments are served afterwards and each parish is asked to supply a plate of nibbles, and, with all these ways of encouraging a number of people to make an active contribution, the benefice services are intended to promote a sense of community across this large rural area.

Due to the challenges created by the ill health that affected some of the ministry team, the broadening of worship styles has not yet taken place. However, the summer has provided some one-off opportunities to try various kinds of creative worship. These have included outdoor 'Praise and Prosecco,' pet services, holiday 'Songs of Praise' and services of choral evensong with visiting choirs from a cathedral and a Cambridge college.

Future plans include updating the services of morning worship and considering café church, along with contemplative worship, and also the re-introduction of a *Book of Common Prayer* service. However, there is a realization that due to age, and other factors, the current ministry team is fragile, and, while the exploration of new vocations is important and encouraging, it will not provide immediate solutions to the limited resources available for leadership and ministry.

3 Some Issues and Questions

Following the three detailed examples of particular settings for planning service patterns, which were described in the previous chapter, we will now draw out and explore a number of the issues and questions which might arise when service patterns are planned and revised.

What are the Rules?

From one point of view, the Church of England is governed by *The Canons of the Church of England*, which includes regulations for the pattern of Sunday worship in parish churches.[4]

Canon B 11 paragraph 1 states:

> Morning and Evening Prayer shall be said or sung in at least one church in each benefice or, where benefices are held in plurality, in at least one church in at least one of those benefices at least on all Sundays and other principal Feast Days, and also on Ash Wednesday and Good Friday.

And Canon B 14 paragraph 1 states:

> The Holy Communion shall be celebrated in at least one church in each benefice or, where benefices are held in plurality, in at least one church in at least one of those benefices at least on all Sundays and principal Feast Days, and on Ash Wednesday and Maundy Thursday

These reflect relatively recent amendments that acknowledge more clearly the now common situation of clergy serving a benefice, that is, a number of parishes and parish churches. They are followed by Canon B 14A, which allows for some flexibility that can be exercised 'on an occasional basis' by the minister and PCC, or on a regular basis with authorization by the bishop. It is this that has been used in recent years to designate some parish churches as 'festival' churches, and allow them some formal exemption from aspects of the Canons, although this seems in practice only to give formal exemption from rules that are widely disregarded in other churches anyway.[5]

It seems obvious that what the Canons set out is not what actually happens in many parish churches, often for very practical reasons, usually relating to resources and numbers of people, but also sometimes for reasons of choice, as clergy and churches simply decide not to observe, in part or in full, what the Canons set out.

If the reality is that we are not in practice governed by these provisions of the Canons, then where should we look for guidance in planning and reviewing patterns of services?

Vision and Values

Many churches will have vision or mission statements, summaries of their values or mission action plans. Any statements or summaries of this kind will be the best starting point for shaping the priorities for that church's worship, whether or not the content of them explicitly addresses the subject of worship. Such a process of reflection could begin by looking critically at the current pattern of services, to see to what extent it actually reflects the stated priorities.

For churches that do not have such statements agreed, it will be harder to find a starting point for identifying the priorities for the worship of that community, and there will be a greater danger of being driven mainly by what has happened before, or what seems possible with the people and resources available at present. However, a group of churches that has no agreed vision could begin by reflecting on their current pattern of services, and asking what values or priorities are suggested or implied by the services they currently hold.

Five Core Values: An Example

When considering the service patterns for a team containing four churches in South Yorkshire, the ministry team came up with five core values they wanted to be reflected across all the churches in their worship:

- *Clearly recognized leadership* (this might involve a key local minister as a focus, as well as a member of the clergy).
- *Maintaining the church's individual identity*, traditions and styles while at the same time...
- *Promoting a team dynamic* and encouraging each church to see itself as a part of the bigger whole.
- *A consistent service time in each church every week,* which required a generosity on the part of congregations to discover a pattern that would work and be sustainable.
- *Proper provision of pastoral care* rather than the vicar rushing off at the end of a service to take another one somewhere else.

Who Decides?

Who is it who holds the power to make the decisions about the service pattern for a group of churches, and to make any changes? Traditionally this would have rested with the incumbent, possibly along with any other clergy involved. Nowadays such discussions would be expected also to involve churchwardens and PCCs. Also many churches now have some form of leadership or ministry team, and they would obviously have a particular role in these discussions as well. However, even where team structures are in place, they do not always function well. A colleague recently told a story about a large rural team ministry, in which a house-for-duty minister independently changed the service arrangements for what he regarded as 'his' church, without any reference to colleagues, which caused enormous problems for the other churches in the team.

It might be a good thing to seek to include the whole congregation in a review and plans for any changes to the service pattern, but this needs to be handled with care, and expectations managed. It is not an easy thing to design an effective questionnaire, and it can be easy to generate large quantities of material that are hard to evaluate, or to draw conclusions from, while people might expect that if they submit their views they will necessarily get what they would prefer.[6]

If service patterns are to be reviewed, and possibly changed, then there is the question of how often this should be done. Sometimes it will be prompted by circumstances, such as a change of incumbent, or pastoral reorganization of parishes, but otherwise there is a balance between being open to change and new things, but not disrupting the pattern too often with successions of changes.

Related to this there is an issue that I have experienced as an incumbent in at least two different posts. When we attempted to review service patterns, I have found that relatively few people other than me actually engage with the complexities of the whole service pattern, but most are focused on their own areas of interest or personal need. These were either their own home church, or the types of services they prefer, or aspects of the worship, such as the choir or music, that they were closely involved in. In one way this is understandable, but I have found that it often leads to people having unrealistic blinkered views or expectations of what could be done, thus often proposing changes and patterns that are simply not possible when viewed in the round.

This leads to the question of whose responsibility it is to hold the overview of the whole pattern. If most people are not in fact going to do that, and perhaps it is not a reasonable expectation to place on them, then whoever does hold the overview will need to be patient in these discussions with others who do not have a grasp of the whole pattern of which their interests and concerns are only a part.

Ministry Resources

The people who are currently available to prepare and lead worship will be a major factor in shaping the pattern of services. As well as the incumbent and any other full time clergy, there might in some cases also be clergy in part-time or house-for-duty posts, along with active retired clergy, and ordained people in other employment who have permission to officiate. For many reasons, the numbers who might be available will vary greatly in different local situations, and in some places there might be larger churches nearby with greater resources, who can help to support other churches around them.

The people who are available to lead worship will be a major factor in shaping the pattern of services

In order to provide for services of holy communion on a sufficiently regular basis, whatever that might be in different contexts, it may be possible to obtain permission for extended communion, to be distributed by a lay minister, but approaches to this, and how readily it is permitted, might vary between dioceses.[7]

There are some who argue for lay presidency at communion, both for theological reasons, and to ease these practical problems, and, while this is possible in some other church traditions, it is not permissible in the Church of England at present.[8]

There will also be authorized lay minsters, notably Readers (Licensed Lay Minsters), and in some dioceses there might be other forms of ministry as well, for example those who are designated as Authorized Preachers in the Diocese of Oxford,[9] or as Authorized Worship Assistants in the Diocese of Norwich, as well as similar schemes in other dioceses.[10] However, even where there are authorized ministers, the extent of their availability, and the roles in ministry that they are suited to carry out, will vary greatly, as will the needs of different churches. For example, some churches will require a leader for BCP evensong, whilst others will require someone to plan and lead all age worship, and one minister might not be suited to both roles.

Many churches will also have other people who, although they might have no formal training or recognition by the wider church, may have an occasional or even a regular role in the planning and leading of worship.

Alongside all of this, the resources available to lead music in worship will also be a significant factor in the number and style of services that are held, whether that is organists or choirs, or worship leaders and music groups, and also how much use is made of recorded music and singing.

How Many Services to Lead?

There is an important question concerning the number of services it is reasonable for one person to take on a Sunday. There does not seem to be any clear standard answer to this question, and the response will vary in part according to what different clergy feel is reasonable for them, as well as depending on the pressure of expectation of the clergy in different churches and groups. This issue is often focused on incumbents and full-time clergy, but might also be a concern for part-time and house-for-duty clergy, as well as for some lay ministers, perhaps especially those who have a role as the focal minister for a local church community.

The pattern of services will often tend to run at the full capacity of those who are currently available, and it can be a challenge to sustain a pattern whenever any regular ministers are lost. This might be especially challenging when a key voluntary unpaid minister steps down, as they will not necessarily be replaced, in the way that a paid minster often will be.

An Example of Coping with Changing Resources

When the staff changed—one Reader retired and moved away—he was married to an authorized lay pastoral minister who also led services; at the same time one of our other Readers died unexpectedly in a road traffic accident. This made a huge impact on the arrangement of services across four churches, which became unsustainable.

It might well be true that our churches are often not very good at succession planning, and often do not look ahead towards replacing the current ministers in due course, even where there is a wish to sustain the current full pattern of services if possible.

What is Fair?

This can be a more complex question than it at first appears. In a group of churches, it might seem fair to try to offer exactly the same ministry resources and number and variety of services to each church, but that might not always be the best approach. But if these things are planned to vary between different churches because of size of congregations or communities, the suitability of different buildings, or a deliberate focusing of resources on particular churches and services because of priorities for mission, then who will decide what is a fair arrangement for all concerned?

A Post-COVID-19 Example

In a team of four churches, due to the sizes of the different buildings, we only used two churches for a while post-COVID-19, because they were the only two buildings large enough for the congregation to socially distance. The two smaller churches were without services for over a year. From some points of view it was not fair, but it was necessary for a season and everyone understood the reasoning.

What Types of Service?

The range and variety of types of worship included within a pattern of services will be hugely varied in different places. Without trying to list all the possibilities here, these might range from traditional *Book of Common Prayer* services, which still have a regular place in some church communities, to more or less formal services of Holy Communion, through the whole range of 'family' or all age services, to more contemporary styles of worship, and recent developments such as Messy Church, café church and Forest Church. There will also sometimes be very particular and distinctive styles of service that belong to a local area, or just to one church.

When a service pattern is being reviewed, it might well be worth taking some time to reflect on the story of what has led to the current pattern of services, in order to be better placed to see whether it is the right pattern to serve the current needs of the churches, or what new opportunities there may be for the future.

Another question, which will be part of the considerations in many places, is the ongoing place of online worship in any form, since the steep learning curve we all shared during lockdown. Some churches have gone back to entirely in-person worship, while some have continued to offer online worship in some form. Some have the resources to sustain high quality video presentations, but for others it might be a simple Morning or Evening Prayer or perhaps Compline, frequently led by lay people, and using relatively simple technology such as Zoom. In whatever form, this might help to make some experience of worship accessible to those who are less mobile or housebound, whether temporarily or for the long term, and might also help members of a church who are away from home still be able to connect the worship of their home church.

Baptisms

One particular question will be how baptisms can be accommodated within a demanding and complex pattern of services, in which ordained ministry is limited. While understanding the value of the principle that baptisms should usually take place within a congregational service, rather than as a separate occasion, it has often been my experience that this can be very difficult to achieve in practice in some settings.[11]

It might be easier to plan to include baptisms when they come in fairly regular and predictable numbers, but this is harder to do when requests for baptisms come in an irregular and unpredictable pattern, as they may in smaller rural parishes. This will also depend in part on the attitude of the families enquiring about baptism, as there might be some who demand the particular date that they would prefer, whilst failing to appreciate the practical challenges faced by the local congregation and clergy.

When there is just one service in each church each month which is of a type and at a time which will suit a baptism being added to it, it can sometimes be hard to find a date that will suit a family party that is not many months away. The result might be that baptisms are sometimes held at a different time outside the regular services, although efforts can still be made to connect the family with the regular congregation.

Major Festivals

In any context there will be a particular challenge around major festivals, when even congregations that have very few services on a regular basis might understandably want to have a service in their own church building, and churches that often have services at less popular times might also want a service at a more popular time on this occasion.

In the approach to Christmas, carol services can be a challenge for the resources of organists and choirs, although the problem can be reduced by inviting other musical groups, such as a local brass band or a school orchestra, to accompany a carol service. At the same time, midnight and other Communions at Christmas might be a challenge to resource from the number of ordained ministers available. At Easter, it is understandable that many congregations would like to have a Communion service, and so there is a similar challenge of providing for all the services and times that people would like.

In some communities there are other occasions in the year, such as Remembrance Sunday, which might also raise similar challenges, especially as many churches will have an expectation of a service around 11.00am. This can be eased if people are prepared to have joint services, or hold some services at other times, but there is often resistance to those ideas.

In the light of all this, some of us remain very grateful every year that there is not a set date for Harvest Festivals!

Joint Services

It is common in many groups of churches to have joint services for all their congregations together, although the frequency of these might vary a great deal in different contexts. It often seems to be a challenge to encourage people, perhaps especially in village communities, to travel away from their own church and village to join services elsewhere. What is planned in a pattern of services with the intention of it being a large and encouraging gathering together of people from various churches might sometimes turn out to be a congregation of the host church along with others who have particular roles and tasks in the worship, while many others from other churches might have treated it as an opportunity for a Sunday off from going to church.

This does not always happen, and there are positive examples of groups of churches that have made joint services work very positively, as a colleague writes:

> We have built up a good solid core congregation who are prepared to move round the benefice week by week. This ensures that the two smaller churches/congregations of the four have a good-sized congregation each time (c 20–30 rather than c 6–10). Building a more team-oriented mentality and an attitude of generosity has helped the smaller village churches thrive.

Consistency and Variety

There have been occasions when dioceses, and local groups of churches, have put a high value on having a service in each place at a consistent time every Sunday. There are ways in which this might be possible, but it has to come at some cost in many situations. If clergy and lay ministers are to lead worship in more than one church, then some churches will always have to hold their services at less popular or convenient times. Otherwise, by using local lay leaders as broadly as possible, most or all churches might be able to hold their services at more popular times, but the cost of this priority might be that incumbents and other clergy are rarely able to be present at services, and opportunities for communion services might be rare.

Travelling

The practical issues of ministers travelling between churches to lead two or more services will vary depending on the distance between communities, and also on the kind of roads and journeys involved. Crossing major roads that are busy with fast long-distance traffic will be one kind of problem, while narrow country lanes, sometimes busy on Sundays with horse riders and cycling clubs, will be another.

There are rural areas with long distances between churches where it is simply not possible for one person to travel between churches to lead more than one service, at times which will be acceptable to the congregations. For example, there are coastal parishes in Cornwall where a benefice runs along the coast but each church is at the end of a long narrow lane with no quick route to the next church despite the fact that as the crow flies it is only one or two miles away, but might be as much as ten miles by road. There is a similar problem in parts of Cumbria with mountains between churches and only limited road access. In response to this and other challenges, the Diocese of Carlisle has adopted an ecumenical approach under the title 'God for All,' supported by four partner denominations with 35 mission communities across the county and together with other fresh expressions.[12]

There should be a concern for the well-being and safety of those who are travelling between churches under these pressures, and at times it might be important to manage the expectations on them, and to remember that keeping everyone safe is more important than being precisely on time under these circumstances.

Of course our churches are being encouraged to take climate change and the care of the environment more seriously, and there is much attention to the energy efficiency of our church buildings and clergy houses. When it comes to travel, I have known a few colleagues in ministry who like to cycle between services when it is feasible. I always enjoy walking, and I do enjoy some occasional opportunities to walk to a church where I am leading worship, usually just in the village where I live, but occasionally, when I have enough time, I like to walk to a neighbouring village and back again. But these opportunities are limited, and, given the expectations of the number, location and timings of the services that many of us are leading, we are likely to continue to be mainly dependent on using our cars.

Communication

Publicity and communicating clear and accurate information about services and other events is always a very important concern, and especially when the pattern of services in each place is varied and complex. It is noticeable how in recent years the amount of printed paper information, in magazines, newsletters and information sheets, has decreased greatly, and some churches do not produce them at all. Information on display boards outside church buildings is still important, but is probably used by fewer people than in the past.

The internet or social media will now be accessible to most people, although it might be challenging in very rural areas, so they have come to play a vital role. It will be important to make good use of websites, email, Facebook, WhatsApp and whatever else will work best in different contexts. Some people prefer to have clear information well in advance, while others prefer reminders nearer to the time of events. Of course there will remain a limited, but important, group of people who for whatever reason do not use the internet or social media, and their needs have to be borne in mind as well.

This area will probably continue to change as there are new developments in technology, and particular forms of social media go in and out of fashion, and are appropriate for different local communities and networks. But, where service patterns have to be varied and complex, it will be very important to make clear and accurate information as widely available as possible.

Stopping and Starting

In seeking to change and develop a pattern of services there will always be the twin challenges of how to stop doing any form of service that has been a regular part of the pattern, and how to clear time and resources to try something new and different.

Churches are very often conservative about change, and sometimes particular services that now attract very few worshippers might still have a small but loyal band who are determined to keep 'their' service going at all costs, and can sometimes be resistant to all change. There are ways that this kind of situation can be addressed, but it is rarely easy to resolve.[13]

Although it might be hard to make the space, and to free up resources, to try something different, it might open up positive new opportunities, and be encouraging and enjoyable, whether or not the first attempt is a complete success. In the next chapter we will look at a few ideas and opportunities for trying something new.

4 Exploring New Opportunities

In the previous chapter we acknowledged many issues and challenges that arise in the process of planning and reviewing our patterns of services, and the difficulties that might come with trying to make changes to an established pattern. However, even when resources are limited, there might still be opportunities, on however large or small a scale, to explore new ways of doing things. In this chapter we will highlight just a few of the ways that many of us might be able to do that.

One-off Services and Events

Earlier we noted how difficult it can be to make space to try any new forms of worship, but one way of doing this can be to make the most of opportunities to try something different on just one single occasion. Sometimes this might lead in due course to something new becoming a regular part of the ongoing service pattern, but, even if that is not possible, it can still be a helpful and encouraging experience. Also, something that is different from any of the current regular services, and that people might not have tried or experienced before, might help to draw the whole worshipping community together from a team or group of churches.

There are many different possibilities, and we have mentioned some already, but they could include café church, Messy Church, Forest Church, contemplative or silent worship, and perhaps even a revival of more traditional forms of worship. There could be a special service focussed on a link with a particular charity. To give one example, a group of churches could gather together for a celebration of World Environment Day.[14] This immediately makes a connection with sympathetic green interests within the community and also fosters links with local schools which are becoming increasingly environmentally aware. What is already familiar in one setting might be new and fresh in another, and there is never anything wrong with borrowing good ideas from other congregations and churches.

Not Always on Sunday

Over the years churches have become well used to the fact that the best time for children's groups and activities might not be alongside Sunday worship, but at a different time on a weekday. Perhaps there are some settings where the same could apply to a local community's main gathering for worship in the week, and there might be some opportunities to meet on a weekday.

An Example of Weekday Worship

The Sunday congregation at St Andrew's, Brinsworth, near Rotherham, was dwindling as the elderly congregation either died or gradually became less able to get to church early on a Sunday morning. Each Thursday, this church was already open for Coffee Pot followed by Lunch Club with a regular clientele. After much discussion and prayer, a short service was introduced at 2pm. This gentle reflective service, which regularly included Holy Communion, suited everyone much better, including those who simply wanted some quiet space in a busy working week. The service was conducted sitting down in the round, so that those with mobility issues or dementia felt comfortable and included. Although initially there were some comments in the community along the lines of 'The vicar has closed the church!', over time this service became the main weekly service at St Andrew's and the congregation both grew numerically and grew younger. In reality, a dwindling congregation had been replaced by a thriving and growing one, who more than doubled in size over a period of four years.

Making the Best Use of our Buildings

Our church buildings vary in size, and in many other ways, and when we use them regularly we might get stuck in patterns and habits, and be all too aware of what we feel are their limitations. However, rather than just running a similar pattern of services in every church all the time, it can be helpful to think about what different buildings are best suited to, and how we could use them to the best advantage. There can be opportunities for this when we are deciding on the venue for a special service, or a joint gathering for a group of churches.

What might be the best church building for a procession, or for moving around inside a building during a service? What would be the best place for a quiet vigil, or an informal praise celebration, or where could we most easily move between the inside and outside during a service, to spend part of it in the natural world? Perhaps visitors and newcomers could help us to see our buildings in a new way, and to help us find new potential in them.

Using Other Buildings

In many communities great time, effort and money goes into maintaining a traditional church building, and it is good to use them regularly for worship, and to open them to all other appropriate uses when we can. However, there are also times when it might be best to use a different building to gather for worship. School halls, community halls, pubs and other public buildings may all be used for worship gatherings, and there are also times when it might be appropriate to meet in people's homes instead.

In one parish where the church is in a beautiful but somewhat inaccessible setting in woodland outside the village, family services are often held in a new community hall in the village, and at least one Sunday service each year is held in the school hall. Apart from practical access issues, there are some people who might find it difficult to approach a traditional church building, either because of past experiences, or just because it is so unfamiliar to them. They might find it easier to consider joining a gathering for worship in a different kind of building.

Going Outdoors

We might bring something fresh to one of our regular worship gatherings by simply taking it outside, into a churchyard or other nearby setting, and there are various special, and possibly one-off occasions that are suited to being outside—weather permitting. In village communities, there might be the opportunity to hold a Plough Sunday celebration or Harvest Festival on a local farm, and one village church has recently held an open-air service each summer, including a pet service and a 'Pimms and Hymns' service. Churches in seaside settings will have opportunities to hold open-air services by the sea, celebrating Sea Sunday or in support of the local lifeboat and its crew. In every setting, there will be some particular opportunities, and also some occasions when the theme of focus of the worship will suggest that it is appropriate to gather outside.[15]

Creative Approaches to the Seasons

The creative use of buildings can really be exploited during different seasons, sharing out the services around a group of churches whilst playing to the strengths and opportunities afforded by the different buildings.

An Example of a Pattern for Holy Week and Easter

In the Walgrave Benefice, a rural group in the Diocese of Peterborough, the Holy Week services are shared out between the churches, playing to the strengths of each building. The Maundy Thursday Supper followed by Tenebrae is held in a medieval church with flexible seating and AV equipment, where it is possible to use projected visuals and set up tables in a cross formation for a simple supper. The Good Friday meditation on the cross is held in one of the smaller churches which has interesting nooks and crannies for one or two appropriate meditative prayer stations. The Easter Vigil is held at the smallest church which has unusual central aisle pillars and a strong monastic connection. Beginning by kindling the fire outside the church door and lighting the paschal candle outside, and then processing by candlelight into the church. A joint Easter celebration is then held in the biggest church, drawing on all the team's musical resources of organ, music group and singers with seasonal refreshments and an Easter egg hunt in the churchyard. Each church congregation feels included and valued in a unique way, based on what each building has to offer.

Alongside all of this, a Palm Sunday procession has added an ecumenical dimension by walking to the local Baptist church.

Welcoming All Contributions

Another way of refreshing our worship can be to look for a range of creative ways, however grand or modest, to involve a wider group of lay people in contributing to the worship in different ways. Some churches take a clear stance on welcoming and involving people as widely as possible in appropriate ways, including those whose faith is very tentative, and who might have no expressed faith at all. In many churches this has often happened with musicians, and can happen with other contributors as well. Looking more broadly at the life of the church, another opportunity is through Open the Book assemblies. It is possible to invite fringe members interested in drama to come and take part in these dramatized Bible stories. They can then learn more about faith alongside the school pupils, and connections can be made with the worship of the church. People may be nurtured in belonging and discipleship through these relationships, and the church community may receive some enlightening insights into what they are doing, and what they could possibly do, sometimes from unexpected sources.

5 Conclusion

So, having surveyed some examples of the way that service patterns have developed and been revised in several different contexts, we have reflected on a number of issues that are raised by this task, and also noted some of the opportunities for renewing the pattern and range of the worship we plan, lead and share.

If there was a simple one-size-fits-all solution to all the questions and issues we have explored, then somebody would have found it a long time ago. But, although there might be good reasons why particular solutions that work in one setting might not be appropriate in another, there are also many valuable lessons that we can learn from the experience of others. It is also important to be realistic and remember that it is actually not possible to keep everybody entirely happy all the time, and to avoid slipping into trying to do everything, everywhere, all the time, far beyond what we can do well with the resources that are available.

According to the Canons of the Church of England, worship is first and foremost about glorifying God, and then secondly about edifying the people (Canon B 1.2). To 'edify' means to build up in faith, for mission and service, and, while that is not the same as pleasing or placating the worshippers, the quality of our worship does matter. As we approach the planning and reviewing of our pattern of services in any context, that work will best be shaped by the vision and priorities for the whole life of the church in that place.

Notes

1 G Alderson, *Writes of the Church* (Abingdon: Bible Reading Fellowship, 2017).

2 areflexanglican.wordpress.com/sunday-services-3/

3 For more discussion of this see A Atherstone and A Goddard, *'Drink This, All of You': Individual Cups at Holy Communion* (Grove Worship booklet W 250).

4 www.churchofengland.org/about/leadership-and-governance/legal-resources/canons-church-england/canons-website-edition

5 www.churchofengland.org/resources/diocesan-resources/strategic-planning-church-buildings/festival-churches

6 See M Earey, *Evaluating Worship* (Grove Worship booklet W 227), especially chapter four about Local Worship Audits.

7 See P Tovey, *Public Worship with Communion by Extension: A Revised and Updated Commentary* (Grove Worship booklet W 249).

8 See A Atherstone, *Lay Presidency: An Anglican Option?* (Grove Worship booklet W 208).

9 www.oxford.anglican.org/ministry/lay-ministry/authorised-ministry

10 www.dioceseofnorwich.org/mission_and_ministry-mission_and_ministry/lay-ministry/mission_and_ministry-lay_ministry-authorised_worship_assistants/

11 This is discussed in chapter 5, 'The Timing of Baptism' (C Read) in C Read, C Buchanan, M Earey and P Tovey (ed), *Introducing Patterns for Baptism* (Grove Worship booklet W 258).

12 See https://www.carlislediocese.org.uk/god-for-all-strategy/

13 For further discussion of this see J Leach, *Ending Well: How to Close Things Down* (Grove Renewal booklet R 3).

14 See Arthur Rank Centre for worship resources for World Environment Day at: https://arthurrankcentre.org.uk/

15 See C Stanforth, *How to Worship Outdoors* (Grove Worship booklet W 256).